Tiger Talk
Number Fun

Size

Karina Law

W
FRANKLIN WATTS
LONDON • SYDNEY

Contents

Look out for Tiger on the pages of this book. Sometimes he is hiding.

Everything has a size.

Some things are big.

Some things are small.

Same size

These skittles are
the same size.

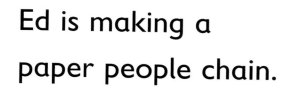

Ed is making a
paper people chain.

He folds the paper.

Now he cuts
the shape.

Look! The paper people
are the same size.

5

Big and small

Anya is
making a
big shape.

Felix is making a small shape.

Big dog · Small dog

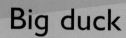

Big duck

Small duck

Which one is the small jigsaw piece?

?

Smallest and biggest

These dolls are all different sizes.

smallest  biggest

smallest

biggest

Can you build a tower using boxes of different sizes?

8

When you blow air into
a balloon, it gets bigger.

small

big

bigger

Tall and short

Rabbit's tower of bricks is tall.

Tiger pushes the tower. Now it is short.

Tiger helps Rabbit to build a tall tower again.

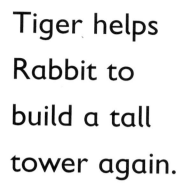

Flowers get taller as they grow.

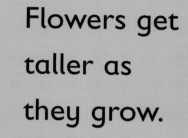

Which of these plants is the tallest?

Different sizes

Our hands grow bigger as we get older.

Rianna and Megan are using their hands to make a handprint picture.

This is a clay hand print.

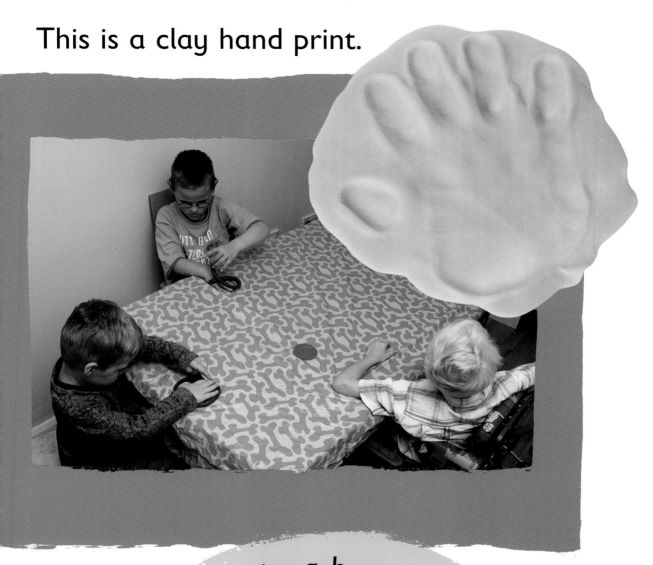

Can you make a hand print like this one?

Long and short

Anya has long hair.

Ed has short hair.

Billy, Harvey and Harrison are making long shapes.

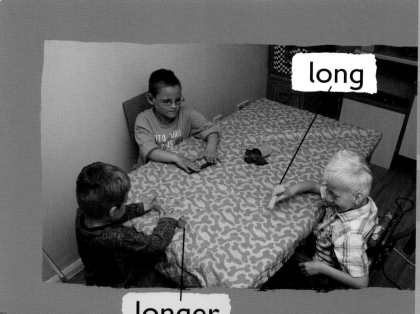

long

longer

Carlo is playing with his trains.

short

long

Which train is the longest?

15

Too big, too small

These trousers are too big.

This jumper is too small.

This hat is too big for Tiger.

Is this bed too small for Rabbit?

Perfect fit

Jenna needs a box for each of these presents.

Which box should she use for each present?

Turn a large box into something else.

Felix can fit inside this box!

19

Measuring

Lots of things can be measured.

weight

length

height

Carlo, Lola and Felix are playing a game.

They measure the
height of the bar.
Then go under it.

Try playing this game.
How low can you
get the bar?

Light and heavy

These
grapes
are light.

This
watermelon
is heavy.

22

Jenna is weighing apples for a fruit pie.

Which fruit is heavier?

23

Word picture bank

Big – P. 3, 6, 9, 16, 17

Height – P. 20, 21

Long – P. 14, 15

Short – P. 10, 11, 14, 15

Small –
P. 5, 6, 7, 8, 16, 17

Weight – P. 20, 23

First published in 2009 by Franklin Watts
338 Euston Road, London NW1 3BH

Franklin Watts Australia
Level 17/207 Kent Street, Sydney NSW 2000

Copyright © Franklin Watts 2009

Series editor: Adrian Cole
Photographer: Andy Crawford (unless otherwise credited)
Design: Sphere Design Associates
Art director: Jonathan Hair

A CIP catalogue record for this book is available
from the British Library.

ISBN: 978 0 7496 8655 0

Dewey Classification: 530.8'1

Acknowledgements:
The Publisher would like to thank Norrie Carr model agency.
Jo Stone, Billy, Grace; Tracey Holyland, Harrison, Harvey; Lisa
Walther, Megan and Rianna.
'Tiger' and 'Rabbit' puppets used with kind permission from
Ravensden PLC (www.ravensden.co.uk).
Tiger Talk logo drawn by Kevin Hopgood.

Leonid Anfimov/Shutterstock: 8t. Eric Isselée/Shutterstock: 7t&tr.
Vasily Kozlov/Shutterstock: 7c&cr.

Every attempt has been made to clear copyright.
Should there be any inadvertent omission please
apply to the publisher for rectification.

Printed in China

Franklin Watts is a division
of Hachette Children's Books,
an Hachette Livre UK company.
www.hachettelivre.co.uk

There are 21 Tigers, including me,
in this book.
Did you find all of us?